BELIEVE
AND

THE WORLD'S MOST
MOTIVATIONAL
QUOTES

ACHIEVE

CHRIS NAYLOR

summersdale

BELIEVE AND ACHIEVE

An Hachette UK Company
www.hachette.co.uk

Summersdale Publishers Ltd
Part of Octopus Publishing Group Limited
Carmelite House
50 Victoria Embankment
LONDON
EC4Y 0DZ
UK

www.summersdale.com

Printed and bound in China

ISBN: 978-1-78685-945-7

Substantial discounts on bulk quantities of Summersdale books are available to corporations, professional associations and other organisations. For details contact general enquiries: telephone: +44 (0) 1243 771107 or email: enquiries@summersdale.com.

INTRODUCTION

Have you ever read an article or watched a TV report about a famous actor, a successful entrepreneur, a tireless humanitarian or a world-renowned scientist and thought to yourself, 'I wish that were me?' If you have, it's safe to say you're not alone. Achievements of any kind help us validate ourselves to others and give us a sense of purpose and worth. For some, little day-to-day victories are enough; others aim for the moon.

But whether it's big or small, success has the same starting point for everyone – self-belief is the spark that ignites your potential. If you believe in your own abilities (or in your potential to better them), and you believe that the goal you're working for is worthwhile, the only things that stand between you and success are time, hard work and perseverance.

This book contains a wealth of inspirational words by people from all walks of life who, in their own way, have found success. Whether they got a lucky break or worked furiously for almost a lifetime, they all share that spark that helped them to first believe and then achieve.

Success is simple. Do what's
right, the right way,
at the right time.

ARNOLD H. GLASOW

IF YOU DON'T LIKE SOMETHING, CHANGE IT.
IF YOU CAN'T CHANGE IT, CHANGE YOUR ATTITUDE.

MAYA ANGELOU

However bad life may seem, there is always something you can do, and succeed at.

STEPHEN HAWKING

Live daringly, boldly, fearlessly.
Taste the relish to be found
in competition – in having put
forth the best within you.

HENRY J. KAISER

SUCCESS IS NOT FINAL, FAILURE IS NOT FATAL: IT IS THE COURAGE TO CONTINUE THAT COUNTS.

ANONYMOUS

DON'T BE AFRAID
TO GIVE UP THE GOOD...

... TO GO FOR
THE GREAT.

JOHN D. ROCKEFELLER

I LEARNED TO
ALWAYS TAKE ON
THINGS I'D NEVER
DONE BEFORE.
GROWTH AND
COMFORT DO
NOT COEXIST.

VIRGINIA ROMETTY

Action is the foundational
key to all success.

PABLO PICASSO

A man who does not think for himself does not think at all.

OSCAR WILDE

THE QUESTION ISN'T WHO IS GOING TO LET ME; IT'S WHO IS GOING TO STOP ME.

AYN RAND

SUCCESSFUL PEOPLE DO WHAT UNSUCCESSFUL PEOPLE ARE NOT WILLING TO DO. DON'T WISH IT WERE EASIER, WISH YOU WERE BETTER.

JIM ROHN

I used to want the words
'She tried' on my tombstone.
Now I want 'She did it'.

KATHERINE DUNHAM

If you wait, all that happens
is that you get older.

MARIO ANDRETTI

MANY OF LIFE'S FAILURES ARE PEOPLE WHO DID NOT REALISE HOW CLOSE THEY WERE TO SUCCESS WHEN THEY GAVE UP.

THOMAS EDISON

WOULD YOU LIKE ME TO GIVE YOU A FORMULA FOR... SUCCESS?

IT'S QUITE SIMPLE, REALLY. DOUBLE YOUR RATE OF FAILURE.

THOMAS J. WATSON

I DO NOT KNOW ANYONE WHO HAS GOT TO THE TOP WITHOUT HARD WORK.

MARGARET THATCHER

Expect problems and eat
them for breakfast.

ALFRED A. MONTAPERT

"

Logic will take you
from A to B. Imagination
will take you everywhere.

ALBERT EINSTEIN

"

IF YOU GENUINELY
WANT SOMETHING,
DON'T WAIT FOR IT —
TEACH YOURSELF TO
BE IMPATIENT.

GURBAKSH CHAHAL

YOU ARE NOT YOUR RÉSUMÉ, YOU ARE YOUR WORK.

SETH GODIN

Take criticism seriously,
but not personally.

HILLARY CLINTON

Develop success from failures.
Discouragement and failure
are two of the surest stepping
stones to success.

DALE CARNEGIE

THE MOST EFFECTIVE
WAY TO DO IT, IS TO DO IT.

AMELIA EARHART

TO CONQUER
WITHOUT RISK...

... IS TO TRIUMPH
WITHOUT GLORY.

PIERRE CORNEILLE

TO LEARN PATIENCE IS NOT TO REBEL AGAINST EVERY HARDSHIP.

HENRI NOUWEN

The most common
way people give up their
power is by thinking they
don't have any.

ALICE WALKER

"

The important thing
is not being afraid to take
a chance. Remember,
the greatest failure is
to not try.

DEBBI FIELDS

"

IF ANYTHING IS WORTH DOING, DO IT WITH ALL YOUR HEART.

BUDDHA

THE FUTURE BELONGS TO THOSE WHO BELIEVE IN THE BEAUTY OF THEIR DREAMS.

ANONYMOUS

I didn't get there by wishing for it or hoping for it, but by working for it.

ESTÉE LAUDER

Act as if what you do makes
a difference. It does.

WILLIAM JAMES

DO NOT WAIT TO STRIKE TILL THE IRON IS HOT; BUT MAKE IT HOT BY STRIKING.

WILLIAM B. SPRAGUE

IF YOU'RE WALKING DOWN THE RIGHT PATH AND YOU'RE WILLING TO KEEP WALKING...

... EVENTUALLY YOU'LL
MAKE PROGRESS.

BARACK OBAMA

CHANGE YOUR LIFE TODAY. DON'T GAMBLE ON THE FUTURE, ACT NOW, WITHOUT DELAY.

Whatever your mind can
conceive and believe,
the mind can achieve.

NAPOLEON HILL

There is no education like adversity.

BENJAMIN DISRAELI

I ALWAYS DID SOMETHING I WAS A LITTLE NOT READY TO DO.

MARISSA MAYER

ALL OUR DREAMS CAN COME TRUE — IF WE HAVE THE COURAGE TO PURSUE THEM.

WALT DISNEY

Instead of wondering when your next vacation is, you ought to set up a life you don't need to escape from.

SETH GODIN

You only have to do a
very few things right...
so long as you don't do
too many things wrong.

WARREN BUFFETT

DEFINE SUCCESS ON YOUR OWN TERMS, ACHIEVE IT BY YOUR OWN RULES, AND BUILD A LIFE YOU'RE PROUD TO LIVE.

ANNE SWEENEY

STOP CHASING
THE MONEY...

... AND START CHASING
THE PASSION.

TONY HSIEH

THE ONLY PLACE WHERE SUCCESS COMES BEFORE WORK IS IN THE DICTIONARY.

VINCE LOMBARDI

Being defeated is often
a temporary condition.
Giving up is what makes
it permanent.

MARILYN VOS SAVANT

"

Entrepreneurs average
3.8 failures before
final success. What sets
the successful ones apart is
their amazing persistence.

LISA M. AMOS

"

SUCCESS IS WALKING
FROM FAILURE TO
FAILURE WITH NO LOSS
OF ENTHUSIASM.

ANONYMOUS

OPPORTUNITIES DON'T HAPPEN, YOU CREATE THEM.

CHRIS GROSSER

Try not to become a person of success, but rather try to become a person of value.

ALBERT EINSTEIN

A successful man is
one who can lay a firm
foundation with the bricks
others have thrown at him.

DAVID BRINKLEY

IT'S ALWAYS TOO EARLY TO QUIT.

NORMAN VINCENT PEALE

LIVE AS IF YOU WERE
TO DIE TOMORROW...

... LEARN AS IF YOU WERE
TO LIVE FOREVER.

MAHATMA GANDHI

LEADERSHIP IS DOING WHAT IS RIGHT WHEN NO ONE IS WATCHING.

GEORGE VAN VALKENBURG

The best way to predict the
future is to create it.

DENNIS GABOR

"

If you're offered a seat
on a rocket ship,
don't ask what seat.

SHERYL SANDBERG

"

WHEN THE WHOLE
WORLD IS SILENT,
EVEN ONE VOICE
BECOMES POWERFUL.

MALALA YOUSAFZAI

IT IS NOT THE STRONGEST OF THE SPECIES THAT SURVIVE, NOR THE MOST INTELLIGENT, BUT THE ONE MOST RESPONSIVE TO CHANGE.

CHARLES DARWIN

The difference between successful people and others is how long they spend time feeling sorry for themselves.

BARBARA CORCORAN

You can never leave
footprints that last if you are
always walking on tiptoe.

LEYMAH GBOWEE

IF YOU DON'T LIKE THE ROAD YOU'RE WALKING, START PAVING ANOTHER ONE.

DOLLY PARTON

IF YOU REALLY
LOOK CLOSELY...

... MOST OVERNIGHT
SUCCESSES TOOK
A LONG TIME.

STEVE JOBS

A MAN WHO DARES TO WASTE ONE HOUR OF TIME HAS NOT DISCOVERED THE VALUE OF LIFE.

CHARLES DARWIN

Only those who
dare to fail greatly,
can ever achieve greatly.

ROBERT F. KENNEDY

"

I was smart enough
to go through any
door that opened.

JOAN RIVERS

"

TO ACCOMPLISH GREAT
THINGS WE MUST NOT
ONLY ACT, BUT ALSO
DREAM; NOT ONLY PLAN,
BUT ALSO BELIEVE.

ANATOLE FRANCE

A DREAM DOESN'T BECOME REALITY THROUGH MAGIC; IT TAKES SWEAT, DETERMINATION AND HARD WORK.

COLIN POWELL

It's more important to
stand for something.
If you don't stand
for something,
what do you win?

LANE KIRKLAND

If you can find a path with
no obstacles, it probably
doesn't lead anywhere.

FRANK A. CLARK

ONLY THROUGH
EXPERIENCE OF
TRIAL AND SUFFERING
CAN THE SOUL BE
STRENGTHENED, VISION
CLEARED, AMBITION
INSPIRED, AND
SUCCESS ACHIEVED.

HELEN KELLER

THERE IS AN OLD
SAYING THAT THINGS
DON'T HAPPEN...

... THEY ARE MADE
TO HAPPEN.

JOHN F. KENNEDY

HAPPINESS IS THE KEY TO SUCCESS. IF YOU LOVE WHAT YOU ARE DOING, YOU WILL BE SUCCESSFUL.

ALBERT SCHWEITZER

Every worthwhile
accomplishment, big or little,
has its stages of drudgery
and triumph: a beginning,
a struggle and a victory.

MAHATMA GANDHI

"

Accept the challenges,
so that you may feel the
exhilaration of victory.

GEORGE S. PATTON

"

YOU CAN'T CROSS THE SEA MERELY BY STANDING AND STARING AT THE WATER.

RABINDRANATH TAGORE

AIM FOR THE MOON. IF YOU MISS, YOU MAY HIT A STAR.

CLEMENT W. STONE

Start where you are.
Use what you have.
Do what you can.

ARTHUR ASHE

We may encounter
many defeats, but we
must not be defeated.

MAYA ANGELOU

EITHER YOU RUN THE DAY OR THE DAY RUNS YOU.

JIM ROHN

KNOWING IS NOT ENOUGH; WE MUST APPLY...

... WILLING IS NOT
ENOUGH; WE MUST DO.

BRUCE LEE

SETTING GOALS IS
THE FIRST STEP
IN TURNING THE
INVISIBLE INTO
THE VISIBLE.

TONY ROBBINS

Keep your eyes on the stars,
but remember to keep
your feet on the ground.

THEODORE ROOSEVELT

"

Never give up... for that's
just the place and time
that the tide will turn.

HARRIET BEECHER STOWE

"

SUCCESS IS A STATE
OF MIND. IF YOU WANT
SUCCESS, START
THINKING OF YOURSELF
AS A SUCCESS.

JOYCE BROTHERS

BELIEF IN ONESELF IS ONE OF THE MOST IMPORTANT BRICKS IN BUILDING ANY SUCCESSFUL VENTURE.

LYDIA M. CHILD

The secret of getting ahead is getting started.

MARK TWAIN

Let me tell you the secret
that has led me to my goal.
My strength lies solely
in my tenacity.

LOUIS PASTEUR

ONE FAILS FORWARD
TOWARD SUCCESS.

CHARLES KETTERING

SUCCESS IS A LOUSY TEACHER...

... IT SEDUCES SMART
PEOPLE INTO THINKING
THEY CAN'T LOSE.

BILL GATES

EVERY GREAT DREAM BEGINS WITH A DREAMER.

ANONYMOUS

In a world that's changing really quickly, the only strategy that is guaranteed to fail is not taking risks.

MARK ZUCKERBERG

"

Opportunities multiply
as they are seized.

SUN TZU

"

DON'T WATCH THE CLOCK; DO WHAT IT DOES. KEEP GOING.

SAM LEVENSON

IT IS STRANGE THAT ONLY EXTRAORDINARY MEN MAKE THE DISCOVERIES, WHICH LATER APPEAR SO EASY AND SIMPLE.

GEORG C. LICHTENBERG

We know what we are,
but know not what
we may be.

WILLIAM SHAKESPEARE

Sometimes you can't
see yourself clearly
until you see yourself
through the eyes of others.

ELLEN DeGENERES

THE ONLY WAY OF DISCOVERING THE LIMITS OF THE POSSIBLE IS TO VENTURE A LITTLE WAY PAST THEM INTO THE IMPOSSIBLE.

ARTHUR C. CLARKE

THE ONLY LIMIT TO OUR REALISATION OF TOMORROW...

... WILL BE OUR
DOUBTS OF TODAY.

FRANKLIN D. ROOSEVELT

YOUR PRESENT
CIRCUMSTANCES
DON'T DETERMINE
WHERE YOU CAN
GO; THEY MERELY
DETERMINE WHERE
YOU START.

NIDO QUBEIN

Don't worry about
people stealing an idea.
If it's original, you will have
to ram it down their throats.

HOWARD H. AIKEN

"

We are the change
that we seek.

BARACK OBAMA

"

IF YOU SEE A BANDWAGON, IT'S TOO LATE.

JAMES GOLDSMITH

A LOT OF PEOPLE ARE AFRAID TO SAY WHAT THEY WANT. THAT'S WHY THEY DON'T GET WHAT THEY WANT.

MADONNA

Let him who would enjoy a good future waste none of his present.

ROGER BABSON

When something is important
enough, you do it even if the
odds are not in your favour.

ELON MUSK

SUCCESS SEEMS TO BE CONNECTED WITH ACTION. SUCCESSFUL PEOPLE KEEP MOVING. THEY MAKE MISTAKES, BUT THEY DON'T QUIT.

CONRAD HILTON

THE WAY TO
GET STARTED...

... IS TO QUIT TALKING
AND BEGIN DOING.

WALT DISNEY

I DWELL IN
POSSIBILITY.

EMILY DICKINSON

If you really want
to do something, you'll
find a way. If you don't,
you'll find an excuse.

JIM ROHN

"

Winners take time to relish
their work... scaling the
mountain is what makes
the view from the top
so exhilarating.

DENIS WAITLEY

"

YOU ARE NEVER TOO OLD TO SET ANOTHER GOAL OR TO DREAM A NEW DREAM.

LES BROWN

YOU DON'T LEARN TO WALK BY FOLLOWING RULES, YOU LEARN BY DOING AND BY FALLING OVER.

RICHARD BRANSON

You shouldn't go through life with a catcher's mitt on both hands; you need to be able to throw something back.

MAYA ANGELOU

Control your destiny or
someone else will.

JACK WELCH

THE ONLY PERSON
YOU ARE DESTINED TO
BECOME IS THE PERSON
YOU DECIDE TO BE.

RALPH WALDO EMERSON

DON'T JUDGE EACH
DAY BY THE HARVEST
YOU REAP...

... BUT BY THE SEEDS
THAT YOU PLANT.

ROBERT LOUIS STEVENSON

DON'T FIND FAULT, FIND A REMEDY.

HENRY FORD

Innovation distinguishes
between a leader
and a follower.

STEVE JOBS

"

It takes courage to grow
up and turn out to be
who you really are.

E. E. CUMMINGS

"

TO THE DEGREE WE'RE NOT LIVING OUR DREAMS, OUR COMFORT ZONE HAS MORE CONTROL OF US THAN WE HAVE OVER OURSELVES.

PETER McWILLIAMS

IT IS BETTER TO FAIL IN ORIGINALITY, THAN TO SUCCEED IN IMITATION.

HERMAN MELVILLE

The great accomplishments
of man have resulted from
the transmission of ideas
and enthusiasm.

THOMAS J. WATSON

Success usually comes
to those who are too busy
to be looking for it.

HENRY DAVID THOREAU

I AM A GREAT BELIEVER IN LUCK, AND I FIND THE HARDER I WORK, THE MORE I HAVE OF IT.

THOMAS JEFFERSON

PEOPLE MAY HEAR
YOUR WORDS...

... BUT THEY FEEL
YOUR ATTITUDE.

JOHN C. MAXWELL

I OWE MY SUCCESS
TO HAVING LISTENED
RESPECTFULLY TO
THE VERY BEST
ADVICE AND
THEN DOING THE
EXACT OPPOSITE.

G. K. CHESTERTON

All progress takes place outside the comfort zone.

MICHAEL JOHN BOBAK

"

Don't let the fear of losing
be greater than the
excitement of winning.

ROBERT KIYOSAKI

"

LONG-RANGE PLANNING WORKS BEST IN THE SHORT TERM.

DOUG EVELYN

YOU MAY HAVE TO FIGHT A BATTLE MORE THAN ONCE TO WIN IT.

MARGARET THATCHER

In order to succeed,
we must first believe
that we can.

MICHAEL KORDA

Luck is what happens
when preparation
meets opportunity.

SENECA

YOU MISS 100 PER CENT
OF THE SHOTS
YOU DON'T TAKE.

WAYNE GRETZKY

IF YOU WANT
SOMETHING NEW...

... YOU HAVE TO STOP
DOING SOMETHING OLD.

PETER F. DRUCKER

ONCE YOU FREE
YOURSELF FROM
THE NEED
FOR PERFECT
ACCEPTANCE,
IT'S A LOT EASIER
TO LAUNCH WORK
THAT MATTERS.

SETH GODIN

Success is often achieved by those who don't know that failure is inevitable.

COCO CHANEL

**One finds limits
by pushing them.**

MICHAEL POSNER

IF WE COULD CHANGE OURSELVES, THE TENDENCIES IN THE WORLD WOULD ALSO CHANGE.

MAHATMA GANDHI

WE ARE WHAT WE REPEATEDLY DO. EXCELLENCE, THEN, IS NOT AN ACT BUT A HABIT.

WILL DURANT

Opportunity is missed
by most people because
it is dressed in overalls
and looks like work.

THOMAS EDISON

Far and away the best prize that life has to offer is the chance to work hard at work worth doing.

THEODORE ROOSEVELT

NOTHING IS IMPOSSIBLE, THE WORD ITSELF SAYS 'I'M POSSIBLE'!

AUDREY HEPBURN

If you're interested in finding out more about our books, find us on Facebook at **Summersdale Publishers** and follow us on Twitter at **@Summersdale**.

www.summersdale.com